CLEVELAND BAY HORSES

FIGURE 1   Cleveland Bay Mares with part-bred foals at foot. A typical scene in the north-eastern Dales country.

CLEVELAND BAY HORSES

ANTHONY DENT

Foreword by
Alexander Mackay Smith, M.F.H.

J. A. ALLEN
LONDON & NEW YORK

British Library Cataloguing in Publication Data
Dent, Anthony
    Cleveland bay horses.
    1. Cleveland bay horse — History
    I. Title
    636.1'4   SF293.C/   77-30580

    ISBN 0-85131-283-7

Published in Great Britain in 1978 by
J. A. Allen & Company Limited,
1, Lower Grosvenor Place, Buckingham Palace Road,
London, SW1W 0EL
and in the United States of America by
Sporting Book Center, Inc.,
Canaan,
N.Y. 12029.

Book production by Bill Ireson.

Printed and bound by The Devonshire Press, Torquay, Devon.

FOREWORD

Most breed histories are written by those heavily committed to the breed in question, as breeders, owners or officers of the breed society. Because of this commitment they are apt to lack the detachment and perspective of the historian. In consequence their works tend to concentrate on pedigrees, on outstanding animals and on those that planned the matings that produced them, giving only cursory consideration to the evolution of the breed as influenced by the changing economies and fashions of domestic livestock as a whole. Such histories are understandably fascinating to those already committed, but are not particularly effective toward arousing the enthusiasm of outsiders who, by becoming breeders and owners, could make major contributions to the breed.

Anthony Dent labours under no such handicap. He is, on the contrary, one of the world's leading hippologists, renowned as co-author of *Chaucer and The Horse* (1959), of *The Foals of Epona* (1962) and of *Animals That Changed The World* (1966). He is also the author of *Donkey* (1972), and translator of the immensely important *They Rode into Europe* by Miklos Jankovich (1971).

Because he was born and brought up in the Cleveland District of the North Riding of Yorkshire, where he now lives (and from which the breed takes its name), Mr. Dent has been able to add his lifetime observations to his talents as a historian, thus producing the best birds-eye history of the Cleveland Bay horse to appear in print.

He begins: "Cleveland Bays belong to a group of breeds known in many European countries as warm-blooded: by which is meant having their origin in a cross of hot-blooded Oriental or Mediterranean stocks (Arab, Barb, Thoroughbred) on the cold-blooded North European horse, such cross, however, being (frequently) of long standing." Present day European warm-bloods illustrated by the German strains (Trakehner, Hannoveranez, Holsteiner, etc.); of France (Selle Français); of Poland (Wielkopoliska); of Hungary (Kisber, Mezlöhegyes, Gidran); and of Russia (Budjonny, Don, Kirghiz). European warm-bloods were cultivated during the 19th-century chiefly for military purposes, as officers' chargers, as troopers' mounts and as artillery horses. Since the armies of their respective countries have become mechanized, however, the European warm-blood breeders have accordingly revised their goals and are now producing horses, not for war, but for sport. To achieve these ends they have not hesitated to bring in outside blood; close-up crosses of Thoroughbred and Arab sires appear in the majority of present-day warm-blood pedigrees. So widespread has the use of Thoroughbred outcrosses become that a group of West German breeders with the backing of that country's largest periodical *(Reiter Revue)* proposes to join all their warm-blood strains under a single Stud Book (as the French have already done) and under a title such as "German Saddle Horse". This practise of using outside blood has unquestionably produced many excellent individuals. At the same time, however, it has produced a decidedly mixed genetic background. A breeder who buys a stallion wants him to be prepotent — to reproduce himself as to type, temperament, soundness and performance. Stallions of the present European warm-blood breeds cannot be relied upon to reproduce themselves solely on the basis of registration in their respective Stud Books — because of mixed ancestry their prepotence is not a breed characteristic, but can only be established for individual stallions through several crops of observable foals.

British breeders, however, have a far different point of view. Because they consider prepotence essential to any breed of livestock, for the past hundred years and more they have maintained Stud Books closed to outside strains. The first volume of the Cleveland Bay Stud Book was published in 1883, and no outside blood has been admitted since. Consequently, if a Cleveland Bay stud colt or stallion meets the buyer's requirements as to conformation and way of moving, the fact that it is registered in the Stud Book will virtually assure its prepotence — its ability to reproduce itself in its foals.

The competitive sport horse of today, in addition to racing, is best exemplified by the three disciplines of the Equestrian Olympic Games — The Three-Day-Event, Show Jumping and Dressage. Since the Speed and Endurance Test on the second day of the Three-Day-Event is given a value of twelve, as compared to three for dressage on the first day and two for Show Jumping on the third, it necessarily follows that Thoroughbred blood, our prime source of speed, is all-important in the Three-Day horse. The speeds required in Olympic Show Jumping also put emphasis on the Thoroughbred. Furthermore, Olympic Dressage requires not only the collection characteristic of such breeds as the Lipizzaner, but also the extension characteristic of Thoroughbred strains.

Thoroughbred blood, except for racing, is not the complete answer to the production of sport horses today, however, even though it is an essential element. For more than 200 years Thoroughbred breeding stocks have been selected for one factor only — speed on the race course. If a stallion or mare will transmit speed to their offspring they will be put to stud, without regard to such considerations as conformation, soundness of wind, limb and temperament, or ability to carry weight. In consequence the Thorough-bred breed as a whole is riddled with unsoundness. The racehorse is asked to carry generally not more than 130 lbs (59 kgs), over a specially prepared level surface, with low ("daisy-cutting") action, at top speed, and to expend every ounce of energy to get ahead of the horse in front. By way of contrast the hunter and other sport horses are asked to carry much heavier weights over varied terrain, including fences and other obstacles, with a higher way of going, at more moderate speeds and to wait their turn at fences in the hunting field and in the starting gates at competitive events. The regulations of the International Equestrian Federation (F.E.I.) specify that horses in the Three-Day and Show Jumping events must carry a minimum of 165 lbs (75 kgs). ·

In consequence the breeder of sport horses must look for other blood to cross with Thoroughbred strains, in order to secure the action and size, and the soundness of wind, limb and temperament lacking in the Thoroughbred. It should also be mentioned, as far as jumping is concerned, while the Thoroughbred excels over spread fences and water jumps, that other breeds with higher hock action, such as the Cleveland Bay, excel over vertical obstacles. Mr. Dent's book demonstrates the superior prepotence of the Cleveland Bay as compared to the European warm-bloods. He further demonstrates, not only that the Cleveland Bay supplies the size, soundness and weight carrying ability lacking in the Thoroughbred, but also why Cleveland Bay blood crosses particularly well with Thoroughbred blood. All Thoroughbreds go back in tail female to about 50 foundation mares of the late 17th- and early 18th-centuries, all of which were domiciled in the Vale of Bedale which adjoins the Vale of Cleveland. The example of the racehorses produced by the Bedale breeders necessarily influenced the general purpose horses produced by the Cleveland breeders — Dent notes that the few Thoroughbred stallions appearing in early Cleveland Bay pedigrees carried the best distance (4 mile racing) blood of the 18th- and early 19th-centuries — no Thoroughbred horse foaled after 1820 appears in the Cleveland Bay Stud Books, nor are there any other strains in Cleveland Bay pedigrees to this day. It follows that Cleveland Bays and Thoroughbreds have a unique affinity which has made Cleveland Bay blood the most successful of all strains to cross with the Thoroughbred.

Mr. Dent cites, for example, the many good weight carrying hunters sired by Cleveland Bay stallions out of light-Thoroughbred or near-Thoroughbred mares. He also cites part-Cleveland — part-Thoroughbred horses who have achieved major success in National and International Competition. Harvey Smith's Madison Time, a member of the British Show Jumping Team at the 1968 Mexican Olympic Games; Juliet Graham's Sumatra, 8th in the 1974 Burghley Three-Day World Championships and top Canadian horse in the 1976 Olympic Three-Day-Event at Bromont, Canada; and Rembrandt, a successful competitor at the Badminton and Burghley Three-Day-Events in England, to name only a few. The Cleveland Bay cross with the Thoroughbred at the present time is being used with ever increasing frequency and success — as compared with the European warm-blood cross, the Cleveland Bay provides, not only much more uniformity, but also far more stamina and "bottom".

Mr. Dent's analysis of the origins of the breed is far more searching and informative than any previously published text, while his analysis of the shifting agricultural economic background which has affected the fortunes of the breed over the past 500 years is equally penetrating. His book will undoubtedly command a wide readership, not only among present Cleveland Bay breeders and owners, but also among horsemen everywhere, including those whose enthusiasm for this unique and long established breed will surely be kindled by this absorbing text.

ALEXANDER MACKAY SMITH
Virginia, U.S.A.

CONTENTS

LIST OF ILLUSTRATIONS

List of Illustrations

ACKNOWLEDGEMENTS

The author wishes to thank the Members, Committee and Officers of the Cleveland Bay Horse Society for their ready help in kindly providing access to records, verification of facts, data and illustration material. Readers may obtain further information from the Secretary at the Society's offices, York Livestock Centre, Murton, Yorkshire.

The author also wishes to thank the following for permission to reproduce the Figures, numbers of which are shown in brackets:

Mrs. S. Roberts (2); Scarborough Museum (4, 5); the Walker Art Gallery, Liverpool (6); John Tindale (8, 14); Daphne Machin Goodall (9); Miss R. Kitching (10, 15); Alexander Mackay Smith (12); Monty (13) and Derry Brabbs, Halifax (18). All other Figures were supplied by the Society or are from the author's own collection.

For
JUNE

I

THIS HORSE

Cleveland Bays belong to a group of breeds known in many European countries as warm-blooded: by which is meant having their origin in a cross of hot-blooded Oriental or Mediterranean stock on the cold-blooded North European heavy draught (formerly war) horse, such cross however being of old standing, which usually means in practice going back to the 17th-century. In Chapter IV, I shall identify these hot- and cold-blooded ancestors repeatedly, but they must remain a personal interpretation of traditions for which documentary evidence is scarce.

The Cleveland Bay is the only such breed in the British Isles, where perhaps the closest affinity, though not at all by blood, is with the Irish Draught Horse. Individuals of Cleveland type may be seen on the Continent; largely because Cleveland sires have been exported for a long time now as "improvers". But not exclusively for this reason. Not long ago I saw in the stable of a Dordogne farmer a big bay mare, nearly 17 h.h. with a big black foal at foot. She had black legs and a slightly aquiline nose, and looked for all the world like a Cleveland Bay. I asked where my friend had got the Cleveland Bay.

"Clivland Bée? Connais pas. Elle est inscrite au Stud Book Trotteur Français." (Registered Harness Race Horse).

Later it was explained to me that the Trotteur Français is of multiple origin, the two principal elements in its make-up being American Standardbred and Norman. And this mare

FIGURE 2 A Cleveland Bay stallion, Knaresborough Sir
Robert, ridden here by his owner Mrs. S. Roberts.

represented a throwback to the original Norman (rather than Anglo-Norman) type. Now Normandy is not among the regions to which Cleveland Bays are known to have been exported (though the Norman had a strong cross of Norfolk Roadster). The inference must be that horses of a type all but identical with the Cleveland must have existed in Northern France before the last century, that Age of Stud Books.

Cleveland Bays stand 16 to 16.2 h.h. But height should not disqualify a good sort on short legs.

The colour is bay only: preferably a bright bay, then, in order of esteem, ordinary (mid) bay, dark bay, light bay, all with black mane, tail and legs. Grey hairs in mane and tail do not disqualify, and they are inherent in some strains. White is not admissable beyond a very small star and few grey hairs in heel or coronets. Legs which are bay or "red" below the knee and hocks do not disqualify, but are a fault.

The body is wide and deep. The back should not be too long, and should be strong, with muscular loins. The shoulders should be sloping, deep and muscular. The quarters should be level, powerful, long and oval, the tail springing well from the quarters.

The head, characteristic of the breed, is often rather large, but should be well carried on a long lean neck.

The arms and thighs and second thighs should be muscular, the knees and hocks large and well closed. There should be 9" of flat bone and more below the knee.

The pasterns are sloping, strong, not over-long.

The legs should be clear of superfluous hair and as clean and hard as possible.

The feet must be of the best, and the action true and free, the hoof blue. High action is not characteristic of this breed. The Cleveland which moves well and is full of courage will flex his knees and hocks sufficiently. The action required is free all round, gets over the ground, and fits the wear and tear qualities of the breed: as good as can be given by short legs under a wide well coupled body.

The foregoing descriptions of the ideal characteristics in the Cleveland Bay are taken from the Instructions, slightly abridged, which the Cleveland Bay Breed Society issued for the use of judges in 1919, and the only significant amendment made since then regards the height, which now in practice ranges from 16 to 17 h.h., though there are many who maintain that the latter is really too much. A mature stallion will weigh about 14½ cwt (755 kgs).

This specification was first drafted in the days when military potential was still a factor, and a note was added to the paragraph on action to the effect that the action described, especially at the trot, was the one most suitable for an artillery horse. This was the role in which the breed, in its warlike aspect, excelled, and was only one aspect of the tractive power of the purebred Cleveland which worked in the traces at speeds greatly exceeding those that could be attained by the only other class of horse capable of pulling the same weight.

The purebred Cleveland today still exhibits these qualities in harness, and the powerful loins, which are the legacy of forebears that could carry 7 cwt (357 kgs) across a pack-saddle, are transmitted in the first and second cross with the Thoroughbred to hunters which make light work of a 2 cwt (100 kgs) rider.

Trotting potential, arising out of the conformation of the hocks and quarters, is often allied to jumping potential, and this is true of the Cleveland Bay, making it a valuable source of blood for breeding show jumpers; for event horses of International and Olympic standard; and with several top crosses of Thoroughbred blood, for steeplechasers.

Hunt Cliffe

Seton

Seasfold

Clayton

Holme

Bellasis

Billingham

Norton

Stackton

Elton

Preston

Eggs Cliff

Easeby

Darlington

Faceby

Carleton

Bushby

Wharleton Cast or Whorlton

Harlsey Cast

Arncliffe

Welbury

Seamer

Scuterskell

Dromonby

Kirkby

Brough

Ingleby

Westerdale Chap

Batterby

Easby

Bilsdale

Barnsdale

Farndale Chap

Chap

R Y

W Cotham

Kirk Lietham

E Cotham

Redkar

Marsk

Yarby

Ylotham

Wilton Cast

Liaseby

Skinningrave or Skengrave

Bratton

Skelton Cast

Kilton Cast

Loftas

Gisborough

Morsham

Nutton

Pinchingthorp

LAN G

Newton

Skelderskew

Kildale cast

Cleve

Locherby

Middlborough

Eston

Ormesby

Normanby

Acham

Morton

Aclam

Tolesby

Staunton

Stansby

Thornby

Nunthorp

Ingleby

Maltby

Nilton

Newby

Aytoh

Stokesley

Millots

Yarum

Tarsall

Kirkwelton

Crathorne

Over Dunsley

Ingleby

Dunsley

Rudby

E Raneton

Appleton

Conyers

W Runeton

Pottoe

Hilton

Dunby

Wolsby hill

Whorlton hill

FIGURE 3 Map of the traditional Cleveland region. Detail from an original engraving *The North Riding of Yorkshire* by Robert Morden.

II

THIS PLACE

Why Cleveland? It has nothing to do with Cleveland, Ohio and very little to do with the Dukes and Duchesses of Cleveland. Cleveland of the bay horses is first mentioned historically in Norse, not English, sources as "Klifland" — the Land of Cliffs, in a double sense. First and most obviously, the rocky steep coastline from the mouth of the Tees to Whitby, and its hinterland, in which there is a second line of cliffs, inland, marking the northeast escarpment of the North Yorks Moors. But dry-land cliffs are common throughout the region: for instance the house where this book is being written is called West Cliff, and facing it across Danby Dale is another farm called East Cliff, both having at their backs craggy walls of rock rising to the brow of the moor. The right name of this Danby is Danby-in-Cleveland, to distinguish it from other Danbys ("Danes' Villages") in the county. But now it is no longer in Cleveland because that name has been bestowed, in the latest reorganization of English local government, on a district, now dignified by the style of county, which is in effect the backyard of industrial Middlesbrough, and more or less corresponds to the conurbation recently known for a short period as Teesside, and including, as the traditional Cleveland never did, a section of the left bank of the Tees River, formerly part of Durham County. Cleveland of the Vikings must in fact have been reckoned to stretch much further south than Whitby, because in the saga account of

22

King Harald Hardrada's ill-fated invasion of England in 1066 mention is made of the sack of Scarborough by the Vikings, as if they had never passed out of Cleveland. In fact the coast between Whitby and Scarborough is traditionally known as the Liberty of Whitby Strand, and it and its hinterland formed the domains of the Abbots of Whitby, a very large complex of estates built up on the original grant of land to the Abbess Hilda by the 7th-century kings of Northumbria. It is worth mentioning this Patrimony of St. Hilda because, as we shall soon see, the Abbots of Whitby may well have been the first systematic horse-breeders in the district.

For a geographical definition of Cleveland as it affects our story it is simplest to regard it as synonymous with the Wapentake of Langbaurgh, a wapentake being what people in the rest of England call a hundred. Its limits are shown on Morden's map of North Yorkshire *(Figure 3)*, drawn at a time just before the Cleveland Bay begins to emerge from the fog of history. An even more rough-and-ready definition is to say that Cleveland is the eastern half of what was the North Riding of Yorkshire, and is now, pending a further stroke of administrative genius, the County of North Yorkshire.

Cleveland, or Langbaurgh, has always been closely linked with Whitby Strand, and at the present time we jointly return a Member to Parliament for Cleveland-and-Whitby: since the Reformation and Dissolution of the Monasteries more than four hundred years ago the lands of St. Hilda have been much less of a state-within-a-state than they had been for the nine centuries before that.

However defined, these two together, Cleveland and Whitby Strand, formed the core or nucleus of a region long famed for a breed of bay packhorses called Chapman Horses in an age when packhorses were of primary importance as the sole practicable, all-season, all-weather means of transport by land. The end of this age was beginning to be apparent in the course of the 17th-century, but it did not quite come to an end until the dawn of the Railway Era, and it was here, in this region on the borders of Yorkshire and Durham, that the sun rose on the first economically viable freight-and-passenger rail system in all the world, steam-powered. But less than a decade after its opening in 1825 the Father of Railways, George Stephenson, laid out another line from Whitby to Pickering, the gradients of which were too steep for steam locomotives to ascend, and for some years the trains on this line were hauled by Cleveland Bay horses.

That Bay Horse region extended northwards as far as Northumberland; westwards as far as the eastern edge of the Vale of York; south to the city of York itself and the Vale of Pickering, to the Yorkshire Wolds, to the flat fens of Holderness beyond them, and thence on into Lincolnshire. (Here the bay horses rubbed shoulders with the Old Black, native to the region surrounding the Wash. It was anathema to the old-time Cleveland breeder, and figures in the double taboo "not a taint of black or blood". The Old Black was rejected because it was too slow, had hairy heels, and was ill adapted for work in hilly country. Not surprisingly, since its ancestral home was Friesland which is almost below sea-level.) On the east it was bounded by the cliffs and the sea, but, as we shall see, salt water has been no obstacle to the expansion of the Cleveland Bay, both into Europe and into other continents.

III

LAND OF BAY HORSES

It is commonplace to say that the characteristic type of a breed is determined by a combination of heredity and environment, and to point to such regions as Exmoor to demonstrate that *only* individuals of the standard Exmoor type could survive in that environment and reproduce themselves. Confronted with a district very similar to Exmoor — of heather covered moors liberally provided with bogs, what woodland there is being confined to the valleys, the maximum altitude being about 1400 feet (430 metres) above sea-level and the sea being very close, to the northeast — one might expect the local breed of horse to be similar also. Cleveland answers pretty well to this description, and yet the horses originating in these two moorland regions are about as different as two breeds can be.

The reason for the difference cannot wholly be laid at the door of heredity. Cleveland Bays are not kept, and never have been kept in all likelihood, in the same manner as Exmoor Ponies with breeding stock running on the moors. All the solid evidence we have from the pre-modern era points to the keeping of some breeding stock under free-range conditions, but on the low ground. However, this practice ceased many centuries ago, and if the brood mares' foals that were to become the famous "Chapman" packhorses, (ancestors on the dam's side of the Cleveland Bay) wintered out, they will have done so in enclosed fields; it is simply not possible in the British climate to maintain horses of this size under "mountain and moorland" conditions. After a few generations they would dwindle to something like average Fell Pony height — say 13.2 h.h. — or smaller.

This is not to say that the Chapman Horse, and after it the Cleveland Bay, was not admirably adapted to *work* in this rather harsh environment. All arable work, over most of the region, made great demands on the joints, the ploughland being a very stiff clay: it was hard work to pull a harrow over it, let alone a plough through it. The Cleveland Bay has no long hair on the fetlock because a horse working this soil with feathered fetlocks would soon go down with "greasy heel". Other than cultivation, the work of the moorland farms for a long period entailed pack-saddle carriage, which demands a very strong back and loins. So also did the commerce and industry of the region, before the railways, because apart from a few main arteries there were for long no paved roads wide enough for a cart or wagon. The only thoroughfares that had an all-weather, all-the-year-round surface were causeways wide enough for pack-horses in single file.

How recent was this era may be seen from the example of Danby parish in which this book is being written. When Canon Atkinson first came to be Rector here, what was called "the Horse Road" over the moors from here to Rosedale was a single row of flagstones 18 inches (50 cms) wide. Canon Atkinson's granddaughter is my contemporary . . . .

Just as important as strong loins, for packwork of this nature, was sound hard feet. These causeways provided a much firmer footing than the main roads of the pre-macadam era, but it was absolutely unyielding. The breeders of the old Chapman, like the old-time breeders of Dales and Fell ponies which worked in similar conditions, rejected white feet, not from "fancy" or because they were an indication of mixed blood, but because white feet mean white hooves, and white hoof is demonstrably softer than black hoof. Traditionally the Cleveland should have "blue" hoof; like the Galloway, and for the same reason. The Cleveland or rather its ancestor the Chapman had to be sure-footed even if it stuck to the causeways because these were full of sharp inclines, and in their uphill and downhill stretches were less like ramps than flights of stairs. One of them that I know well, leading from Grosmont to Whitby through the woods, and known as "The Flags", is in fact just like a stone stairway.

I have seen it asserted that packhorse ancestry, which is common to many light and medium harness breeds, carries with it a long back, because the breeders of packhorses selected long backs as allowing more room for a load. But this is not universally true, and in fact one can often see short backs in purebred Cleveland Bays. This also could be a legacy of the Chapman. It depends what sort of load was to be carried. Of course, light bulky loads demanded a long back over which the load could be spread, and perhaps for purely farm work this type might be favoured. But there has been, off and on, very considerable pack traffic in minerals in the Cleveland region as a whole: for instance a track across the moors just outside the intake wall of the farm where I am writing now was for centuries used to carry lime from the southern escarpment overlooking the Plain of York to the limeless coastal region near Whitby and, likewise, soft coal (lignite) from the long since played-out pits on the crest of the moor down to the furnaces where the lime was burnt. So the carriers would also have need of a horse with a short strong back across which anything from 2 cwt (102 kgs) to 4 cwt (204 kgs) of lime or coal could be slung in a very small compass considering its weight.

Consider only one industry which was important in

Cleveland from the 17th- to the 19th-century — the alum trade. The finished product had to be got down to the coast for export, even if that "export" was only by coasters to East Anglia or London. Some of the alum was mined on the seashore itself, but some of the quarries were inland. In any case the processing took place at the coast: it was complicated, involving roasting and then slaking the ore, and there were some trains of packhorses carrying the heavy ore, and others carrying the much lighter and bulkier brushwood to stoke the fires. Again, the packhorses served the iron works which operated in Cleveland in small units from medieval times until the Industrial Revolution. The iron was smelted at the pit-head, with charcoal which is a typical light-bulky load, and carried away in the form of pigs, a heavy concentrated load.

And it is iron which brings us, again, to the question of environment. The strongest determining factors in the latter, weather apart, are the soil, on which the quality of natural herbage depends, and water. Over the region as a whole the soil is deficient in lime but the water is heavily charged with iron. In some streams into which the drainage was pumped from the ironstone pits that were still working in my youth, the concentration was so strong that it was lethal to fish, there was a bright orange silt, and stock could not be watered from the beck. But even where the seepage is only natural, as in the stream off the moor that waters our fields here, there is enough iron in the water for the rust-red sludge to be visible to the eye when we come to clean out the stone troughs in the fields. Iron is a most valuable trace element and if not present naturally in the feed or water has to be supplemented. It is worth thinking how much the constitution of the Cleveland Bay has been determined by generations of mares taking in a great quantity of iron in their daily waterings, and what will be the long-term effects

FIGURE 4 Packhorses at Scarborough Spa. Detail from an original engraving *Prospect of Scarborough* by Francis Place, 1731.

of the lack of this in other regions — such as parts of the United States — where their descendants carry on the race quite unmodified so far as introduction of alien blood is concerned, but surely very slowly mutated by the long-term effects of a change of soil and water.

It is of course difficult to form a picture of the make and shape of any local breed during what we may call the formative period of the Cleveland Bay, from sheer lack of artistic representations unequivocally identified as Clydesdale, Norfolk Roadster or what have you, and the formative period in this instance is the early 18th-century. Of this vintage I have only seen two engravings that have any relevance. Both are views of Scarborough beach in the 1730s and are illustrated here *(Figures 4 and 5)*.

The first, *Prospect of Scarborough* by Francis Place, shows two Chapman packhorses carrying compact heavy loads, ankers of mineral water from the Spa. The second shows fashionable holidaymakers disporting themselves on the seashore, bathing, riding, driving, going for a picnic in a coach, and is by J. Settrington. It is a pity that the latter did not get into his picture the horses that drew the "bathing machine" seen in the foreground, since they ought to be identical in type with the water-carriers. But the others seem to be all of one pattern, and show the varied use to which the local horses were put. They also illustrate the limitations imposed by the standard of road building at that time. The man in the one-horse post-chaise has brought it down to the shore for a spin because between the Spa and the Old Harbour there is about 5 furlongs (1000 metres) of level sand, firm at the right stage of the tide, more suitable for trying out the prowess of this horse at a smart trot than any kilometre of metalled road in the district. It was for just this reason, at just this period, that the eccentric squire of Skelton Castle, John Hall Stevenson, friend and patron of the novelist Laurence Sterne, used to try out his coach teams on Saltburn Sands at the other end of the Cleveland coastline.

At a later period, which coincides with the great period of English sporting art, problems of a different nature arise. There is no lack of paintings, and engravings reproduced from them, done at the end of the 18th- and the beginning of the 19th-century. But by this time the type of the Thoroughbred had become fixed, its outline was engraved, so to say, on the brain of every painter whose speciality was horses, and it became the *beau idéal*, in terms of horseflesh, not only in the British Isles but over most of Europe. The overwhelming number of pictures of carriage horses were commissioned by the owner, and the great temptation to the artist was to paint not what he saw, but what he thought the owner wanted to see. On this point we have evidence of the great wood-engraver Bewick, who gave up this sort of work as soon as he could afford to do so, on grounds of integrity. On the strength of art work dating from this period one gains the impression that there must have been, since about the end of George II's reign, a very strong infusion of Thoroughbred blood in the Cleveland, but the evidence of written pedigrees is to the contrary, as also is the old breeders' slogan "free from taint of black or blood".

In my view, too literal credence should not be given to paintings of this breed done in the Romantic period, since the artist may well have pandered to the unspoken wishes of the owner, and given his bay horse more of a Thoroughbred look than it actually had in life.

James Ward seldom succumbed to this temptation, and did not do so when commissioned by Rowland Alston, M.P., to paint his Cleveland Bays, Blucher and Reformer. Ward's painting was exhibited at the Royal Academy in 1836. The Cleveland Bay Stud Book records stallions 251 Reformer who travelled in 1833 and 39 Blucher who was foaled in

FIGURE 5 Carriage and saddle horses on Scar

From an original engraving by J. Settrington, 1735.

FIGURE 6 From the painting *Three Brood Mares*, by George Stubbs (1724-1806). A recent veterinary examination of this painting showed the bay horse on the left to be a colt. The two chestnut mares are Thoroughbred, or nearly so, and the Cleveland Bay colt has been turned out with them with a view to getting Yorkshire Coach Horses.

1822. If these are not portraits of them, they will be of geldings by them, for it was all too bafflingly common to name a colt after his sire, without adding II, or even Young (the Stud Book has three Duke of Clevelands foaled between 1849 and 1864). The reader may judge for himself how closely these horses resemble the description of the right old type of Cleveland from reproductions of this painting which are easily accessible (it was for instance a commercial Christmas card in 1974). The original is in the Paul Mellon Collection at Washington, D.C. in America. (Owing to a temporary change of policy, authority to reproduce the painting at the time of going to press was unobtainable.)

George Stubbs, of equal integrity and even greater objectivity has left us in *Three Carriage Horses* (Walker Art Gallery, Liverpool), the subjects of which are not identified by name, at least one (the horse on the left) realistic impression of the Cleveland horse of the same period as can be seen in the illustration *(Figure 6)* reproduced on the opposite page.

IV

THE ANCESTORS

Having come down to a point at which the type of the Cleveland Bay had been fixed for more than a century — slightly longer than the corresponding period in the evolution of the Thoroughbred — it is appropriate to look backward and consider the nature of the two elements mentioned at the outset of this book whose synthesis of cold- and hot-blood made up the durable, stable, true-breeding warm-blood amalgam.

The cold-blood was the Chapman Horse, a weight-carrying packhorse of great stamina in terms of distance, but also by the nature of the traffic compelled to travel at a respectable speed. This was a coastal region, and its principal export, landwards, was fish, from the port of Whitby and neighbouring fishing villages such as Skinninggrove, Staithes, Runswick Bay, Sandsend and Robin Hood's Bay. Unless fish is salted, it is no good carrying it at the speed of an ox-wagon to market. In the days when the English mail coach was the fastest method of transport by land, a great part of its parcel traffic consisted of hampers of fish, and much earlier than that we have a statement by King Henry VIII's Master of Posts pointing out that the "fish rippers of Calais" made better time between that place and Paris than the English mail did between London and Dover. Of course some of the fish *was* salted, a fact which gave employment for more packhorses though not at such an urgent pace, for salt was not produced locally. It came across the breadth of England from Cheshire, and the road to Whitby led over a pass at the brow of the North York Moors that is called to this day Saltersgate.

For about eight centuries before the Reformation the fishery of Whitby had been the property of the Abbey, which needed a fair number (63 in 1394) of packhorses to carry this most valuable asset to market inland. Throughout the Middle Ages the monastic houses of the region were the principal horse breeders for all purposes except purely military, and it is apparent from their records that horses were widely bred, though not in every part of Cleveland and the Liberty.

Of all the lands belonging to Whitby, only a small group of manors in the far south, close to Scarborough, carried any large stock of brood mares (Hackness, Suffield, Everley) and for a long period tenants of the Abbey worked land not for a cash rent but by service on these manors. They had, among other agricultural chores, to "go to stud". This meant rounding up the mares and foals several times a year, but particularly in the autumn, when the foals were all caught up and branded, taken down to the cultivated lands for weaning and the mares turned back on the rough grazing, which was not moorland but fairly sheltered valleys that were gradually being cleared of woodland. A similar type of ground a little to the north of this was used by Whitby Abbey for the same purpose, part of Harwood Dale round about a farm then and now called Keasbeck. The mares and the stallion ran together with a herd of dairy cows, and because of a prolonged lawsuit with Bridlington Priory which also claimed grazing rights on this ground we know that in 1231 the Abbot of Whitby was fairly selective about the stallions used; for after much wrangling he allowed the Prior of Bridlington to pasture his mares there — but not the Bridlington stallion!

The pattern of ecclesiastical horse-breeding is the same

over the whole region, whether it concerns the Benedictines of Whitby, the Austin Canons of Guisborough or the Cistercians of Rievaulx. Large landowners like de Brus of Skelton or de Mauley of Mulgrave were very generous in grants of land to monastic establishments. These took the form, besides the outright gift of freehold — frankalmoin as they called it — of a more restricted endowment in the form of grazing rights. The deeds of these survive, and they specify what sort of stock, and how many head, the beneficiary is to pasture. Whereas the monks were often given the right to pasture sheep on the moorland in numbers like twenty score ewes and followers, specific grants of horse pasture mention much smaller numbers, and *never* on the moor. It is always in the dales, usually towards the dale-head where the best grazing would be in the ever-widening clearings or "riddings" in the woods.

Typical of such grants are grazing for two or three mares with their followers *(sequela)* up to three-years-old, so that the whole band (to use the American term) would not be more than a dozen head all told. Very often the condition is that the stags (three-year-old colts) are to be taken off in the spring. So somebody was concerned with the avoidance of incestuous inbreeding by the colt out of his dam. The inference is, from the nature of the ground so used, that the monks were not interested in producing a Dartmoor/ Exmoor/Welsh Mountain-sized pony which is all that the heather moors would have kept.

It would appear that long before the dissolution of the monasteries the monastic estates had established, as a breed, the female ancestor of the Cleveland Bay, a packhorse but also a general-purpose agricultural horse that was to become known as the Chapman, somewhat like a Dales Pony and not much over 14 h.h. The cold-blood element.

The hot-blooded element, not of native origin, was added

by the landowners among whom the monastic estates were divided at the Dissolution of 1539. Of these we may take as typical the Cholmley family who became the first lay Lords of Whitby Manor. It is convenient because they remained in possession a long time, being still active in the construction of public works and in all kinds of industrial enterprise until the 18th-century.

In practice the hot-blooded horses easiest to come by for English breeders were the Barb and the Andalusian. The true Arab of the desert could only be procured at great cost, and transported home at even greater cost, and then only through the medium of the English Consul at Aleppo: and we have no record of any landowner in this part of the world ever having pulled off such a deal at long range. The same is true of the "Turk" properly so called, an animal somewhat like the modern Akkal-Tekke breed, and only to be purchased at Constantinople itself.

But, during the reign of Queen Elizabeth I, the custom grew up for young gentlemen of affluent parentage to make the Grand Tour of Europe on coming down from university or the Inns of Court. Many of them brought back a Barbary Horse: they would go down to Marseilles where they could buy one, still seasick, on the dock-side for around £100. It was reckoned that keep and stabling on the road across France to Calais would cost another £100: and the fare to Dover, and expenses on the road to the North Country would bring the total outlay up to about £250: but if the tourist rode the horse home himself, he would not count the cost as anything but the bare price of £100, which was reckoned a canny buy. These Barbs were all stallions: there were simply no mares on offer, so that when we read that the Cholmley in possession of Whitby Manor in 1621 had a bald (whitefaced) bay Barbary mare, we can be quite sure that a mare by a Barb out of a local mare is meant.

FIGURE 7 Mare and foal, direct descendants of the first Harpham Turk. From an original painting in the possession of the Cleveland Bay Horse Society.

Since one has seen the assertion in print that somewhere in the unrecorded pedigree of the Cleveland Bay there must be sires descended from the Old English war horse, it is as well here to dispel that illusion.

The breeding of war horses (Great Horses) in feudal times was in effect a Crown monopoly. A system of studs was set up, country-wide, by Edward I about 1290, and for two centuries it supplied the remount requirements of the armoured cavalry. It was ruined almost beyond repair during the Wars of the Roses, the victor of which, Henry VII, would not spend the money required to set it going again. So ruinous was it that when Henry VIII succeeded to the kingdom he devised a new, and notorious, system of legislation whereby the breeding of horses "able for service in the wars" was made the responsibility of certain classes of subject. While the Royal Studs of war horses functioned, the nearest branch of the *service des haras* was well within range of the Cleveland breeder. It was at Pickering; managed by the Constable of the Castle there. It so happens that for a few years in Edward II's time we have the accounts of this Stud, kept in minute detail, down to the price of a can of axle-grease on the expenditure side, and on the income side down to such items as 6d by sale of the hide of a dead foal. Nowhere in these accounts is there any item for the keep of visiting mares under expenditure, nor, under income, anything that can be construed as a stud fee. One can only conclude from this that the services of the royal stallions were simply not available to private owners.

If the old-style charger of the age of chivalry, that ponderous armour-carrier trotting at five miles an hour, played no part in the ancestry of the Cleveland Bay, the new-style charger of the Age of Gunpowder had enormous influence, which reached its maximum just after the mid-point of the 17th-century. This was none other than the famous Andalusian breed of Spain, and after the death of Queen Elizabeth I in 1603 her anti-Spanish policy was turned inside out by her successor James I who assiduously cultivated the amity and alliance of Spain and tried hard to marry his son to the Infanta. The customary exchange of gifts included presents from the King of Spain of large numbers of top-class Andalusians from the Royal Stud at Cordoba, which were placed in the care of the Royal favourite, George Villiers Duke of Buckingham, Master of the Horse, who in 1620 married Lady Katherine Manners, and with her acquired the huge Helmsley estate: so that most of the Spanish gift horses gravitated to the western border of Cleveland. The strict Royal monopoly was a thing of the past now, and Buckingham freely dispensed the favours of his master's stallions. For love when flush, for money when broke.

These favours were worth having. The Andalusian of that time we can see painted as the throne of Royal models for equestrian portraits scores of times over — by Velasquez in Spain, by Van Dyck in England, by the Clouets in France. It was the only European hot-blood, short-coupled, with a superb outlook, around 15 h.h., very massive powerful sloping croup and superbly arched neck. It did not have the speed of the Barb, but it had much Barb blood. It did not have quite the endurance of the Arab, but it had some Arab blood. We should not equate it exactly with the Andalusian of today, which has been much Arabised since about 1900, but it had the teachability and handiness still typical of the breed — a handiness dearly bought in training for, and practice of, the mounted combat (rather than hunting) with wild boars and half-wild bulls that was the supreme test of virility for Spanish hidalgos. Like the Barb, the Andalusian had a tendency to a Roman nose, often very pronounced, and this both hot-blooded ancestors have bequeathed to the

Cleveland. The Andalusian came in all colours, including palomino, but the most frequent were black and bay and of them all the bay was most esteemed.

No European monarch before about 1750 would dream of sitting for his equestrian portrait on anything but an Andalusian — unless it was a Neapolitan or a Lipizzan and both these are Andalusian crosses. Likewise no General from Sweden to Sardinia would appear on the battlefield on anything but an Andalusian, and no Colonel either if he could afford it.

In the Civil War of the 1640s Generals and Colonels sprang up like mushrooms in the English countryside overnight, and the first thing they did was to equip themselves with an Andalusian charger or a plausible imitation thereof. And all entire. Geldings were for troopers, but the proper conveyance for an officer and gentleman was still a stallion, as it had been in feudal times. Now in the dreary decade that followed the war, half these Generals and Colonels became the military governors or the civil administrators of the provinces in that uneasy Commonwealth. Of the other half, the majority who did not go into exile retired to their country estates, keeping what is now called a low profile. All kept their old war horses with them, and now devoted them less to the service of Mars than of Venus.

Of these warriors there was no shortage in North Yorkshire, from the Republican commander-in-chief downwards. Lord Fairfax, quite early in the war had beseiged and reduced Helmsley Castle, and this with its estate now fell into his hands in lieu of his pay which was many years in arrears. Likewise, Buckingham's Spanish horses, or such of them as had survived the war. On the Royalist side Sir Hugh Cholmley of Whitby, famous for his stubborn defence of Scarborough Castle, went into exile but was injudicious enough to return too soon and spent several years of Cromwell's rule in prison. And his horses together with his sequestrated estates fell into the hands of the Republican supplanter. But they did not leave the district. The same pattern was repeated throughout the region — large numbers of (relatively) unemployed Andalusian stallions now for the first time became available to any owner of a Chapman mare.

So now we have had three waves of hot horse-blood beating on the shore of Cleveland — two from Spain and one from Barbary. Unexpectedly after the Restoration came a second from Barbary, perhaps more far-reaching than the others. When Charles II married Catherine of Bragannza, her father, the King of Portugal, gave as part of her dowry the port of Tangier in Barbary. Great hopes of its economic and strategic development were entertained by the English, the more so since Gibraltar was not yet theirs. A deep-water port on the Atlantic side of the straits, commanding the entrance to the Mediterranean, and in the same latitude as the new colony of Carolina, no further away from it than Southampton is from Baltimore, as the gull flies. The possibilities were infinite; once a good harbour had been built. You can read all about it in Pepys' diary. The conditions of tide and current were such that the only people in England capable of carrying out the harbour works required, and chiefly The Mole, were the marine engineers and masons who worked on Whitby harbour. And so the concession to build The Mole went to Sir Hugh Cholmley of Whitby, and he shipped out skilled masons used to getting their feet wet, carpenters and other mechanics, even quarrymen — all from Whitby. A cove just along the coast from Tangier, where stone was quarried for the harbour-works, was actually named Whitby. Whitby ships carried out great quantities of supplies for the garrison, from salt beef and biscuit to clothing and gunpowder and roundshot and boots, and brought nothing back, for trade through the port was non-existent — was never to develop, in English hands. So all these ships came back in ballast. Now was the opportunity for Cleveland breeders to buy Barb horses direct from the Moors, or from the garrison (the Tangier Horse and the Tangier Foot) who often had prizes of war taken from the raiding Moors and were anxious to turn them into cash to slake the thirst that service in that hot station generated. The opportunity was taken.

That is what people mean when they say that the Cleveland Bay as such — as opposed to the Chapman — was fixed as a breed before the Thoroughbred was so fixed. Because well before the end of Charles II's reign this Andalusian/Barb/Chapman amalgam had solidified: whereas the Great Names which stand at the beginning of the General Stud Book had still to reach England from Vienna and Aleppo and Belgrade and Budapest.

And all the time the Chapman went its separate way, now less exclusively under the pack-saddle than before, for this was an age of moderate but steady progress in agriculture and in road-building, making the use of wagons on the road a possibility. By 1684 the type of plough and wagon harness that was still worked in by Cleveland horses at the dawn of the tractor era was already developed, and here it was already more usual to plough with horses than with oxen, whereas in most other parts of England the reverse was true. We have an explicit statement in George Meriton's *Yorkshire Dialogue* (1684) a sketch about farming in the Northallerton district written in the dialect of the region, about the characteristic method of "yoking" one horse in the plough before a pair: this unicorn formation remained typical of Cleveland practice until World War II. These teams replaced teams of six oxen, being able to pull the same weight but much faster.

While the riding and coach type of Cleveland did not materially alter in the century between 1685 and 1785, the Chapman undoubtedly did. It became much bigger, as a result of better feeding. Of course "gentry" horses in the reign of Charles II got as much oats as they do now. But the farm horses in Meriton's *Dialogue* never get their teeth round an oat. They work on what he calls "hinderends" — something between bran and chaff — which served to bulk out "blendings". The latter was a mixture of dried beans and dried peas, sown and harvested together: high in protein but tending to generate gas in the bowels. The reason was simply that the farmers themselves lived very largely on oats, in various forms from the very solid havercakes (bannocks) through porridge to "cael" which was a kind of gruel that was also fed to weaner calves. The rest of the oats was sold off the farm. But in the following century agricultural improvement provided enough oats to feed farm horses in work and brood mares and young stock also, without depriving the family of their havercake. It must have been some time between the American Declaration of Independence and the end of the 18th-century that the Chapman grew finally to the size of what was known in my father's lifetime as the "agricultural type" of Cleveland.

We may now leave the 17th-century, so momentous in the history of the Cleveland Bay, but not before taking one backward look — in the direction of fox hunting. This sport in a form essentially similar to that of today was carried on much earlier, in this region, than in that area of the Midlands known as the Shires and regarded as the classic English fox hunting district. Notoriously, the Bilsdale is regarded as the oldest established pack of foxhounds in the world and both it and some neighbouring packs, such as the Sinnington, trace their origin to the hounds kept by the Duke of Buckingham — meaning the second Duke. Elder

FIGURE 8 A meet of the Glaisdale Hounds in their native district. These hill farmers are riding pure- and part-bred Cleveland Bays.

son of James I's Master of the Horse, he recovered his sequestrated estates in Yorkshire by the simple expedient of marrying General Fairfax's only child, a rather plain daughter. For a quarter of a century after the Restoration he lived at Court, being noted for his dissipation even among the loose-living boon companions of Charles II. When the latter died in 1685, Buckingham left London never to return, but spent the rest of his life as a country gentleman on the Helmsley estate hunting the fox in Bilsdale.

Hunting at that time was, for the nobility, still essentially the pursuit of edible game and seldom carried out over rough country: there was (fallow) deer hunting in those parks that had survived the ravages of the Civil War, and hare hunting on the open fields. Fox hunting was for farmers. Buckingham was the first peer known to have indulged in it habitually. And to hunt in Bilsdale he could only be mounted on the horse that was master of those steep slopes, those boggy moorlands, those craggy brows and barely fordable becks swollen with the winter rains — the Cleveland Bay such as it had become in the course of his own lifetime. Fox hunting was the death of him — he caught a mortal chill digging out a fox in April 1687.

Now step forward a hundred years. By 1787 Englishmen were living in a different world, transport-wise, from the England of the Duke of Buckingham in which the coach from London took four days to get to York. The mail coach now took twenty hours as a record, and only twentyfour as a regular thing. In fact the stage had been reached where the Cleveland Bay — which in the reign, say, of George II, had had no peer as a coach-horse — was now a fraction too slow for tooling along the new macadamised turnpikes at an overall speed of ten miles in the hour, which in practice means that in places speeds of 20 miles per hour must be achieved. Thoroughbred horses, usually demoted from

FIGURE 9 Two early 19th-century Yorkshire horse-dealers, the sort of men who distributed Cleveland Bays about the country. From Walker's *Costume of Yorkshire*, 1814.

other occupations, were to be seen in the traces of crack mail coaches. And so the Yorkshire Coach Horse came into being. This was not a breed but a cross: usually by a half-bred Cleveland stallion out of a Cleveland mare. To keep the York coach on the road, four-in-hand, changing at stages of ten miles, with reserves, two hundred horses were required. The keep of each cost £2 a week. No wonder the fare, in the 1780s, was 1s a mile — a day's pay for a private soldier, the price of a pound of prime steak, or half a bottle of quite good port. No wonder the demand for coach-horses seemed insatiable, the more so since it was reckoned they only lasted three years on the road.

The Yorkshire Coach Horse easily outlasted the mail coach. In fact, exactly another hundred years on, in 1887, a Yorkshire Coach Horse Stud Book was initiated, which was kept up until 1936. There was much confusion in the public mind, even in England, about the "Yorkshire", called by some the New Cleveland Bay. Some thought it was a separate breed, others that it was simply another name for the same thing. In fact it was neither. Foreigners were totally unable to distinguish between the two, and many so-called Clevelands to be found in the pedigree of Continental coaching breeds were in fact Yorkshire Coach Horses. Examples in the Oldenburg Stud Book are a horse called Luksall (Luck's All) and another called Duke of Cleveland.

Other momentous happenings in the 18th-century were the beginning of Continental expansion of the breed. Before 1760, George II, who was also Elector of Hanover, and his son the infamous "Butcher Cumberland", drafted Cleveland Bay stallions to the Electoral Stud at Celle in Hanover and into that of Oldenburg. The purpose of both these establishments was to horse the carriages of the ruler, and to provide chargers for the military members of the Royal Household and the officer corps generally; in the latter capacity losses initially must have been very heavy, owing to the involvement of Hanover and Brunswick in the Seven Years' War (1756-1763).

At home, a legend grew. The time-honoured boast of the Cleveland breeder has been "free from taint of black or blood". So far as the exclusion of black Lincolnshire carting blood is concerned, this is indisputable, since the cross-breds were so easily identifiable by their white markings on feet and face. But the imprint of intrusive Thoroughbred blood is less obvious. One of its symptoms is "red legs" — the absence of black legs which are part of the true bay pattern — and is usually the legacy of a chestnut Thoroughbred sire somewhere in the family tree. The late Sir Alfred Pease and Major J. Fairfax-Blakeborough, having diligently searched

the records, shed light half a century ago on the Thoroughbred taboo; it was indisputably broken during the 18th-
century. But they were able to define the limits to which this
crossing had gone. All Clevelands then surviving traced back
to no more than seven Thoroughbred horses, of which the
most important were Manica by the Darley Arabian out of
Darley's Jester, and Jalap by Regulus by the Godolphin
Arabian (or Barb, as some say still).

Manica was foaled in 1707 and was thus a senior member
of the first generation of Thoroughbreds born in Yorkshire.
In 1704 Thomas Darley had written to his father,
announcing the purchase of the horse at Aleppo "the name
of the horse is Manaka". More than a lifetime ago now,
Wilfrid Scawen Blunt commented on this name: it was not
that of the individual horse but a free transcription of the
Arabic term *muniqi*, signifying a strain peculiar to Iraq and
of (then) recent origin arising from a cross of Turkoman
blood. In the Orient such *muniqi* horses were used
exclusively for racing; not for hunting or war, and their
forte was speed rather than staying power (but staying
power, to the Bedouin, meant the ability to stay all day and
all night). By contrast with the better-known Seglawi and
Kelilan Arab types, they were long, tall, rather narrow and
slabsided. It is fair to assume that Manica was given his sire's
"middle name" because he so strongly resembled him. And
there are two portraits by Wooton of Darley's Arabian.
Manica cannot have lived long after 1730.

Jalap was a grandson of the Godolphin horse, and was
foaled in 1758, by Regulus out of Red Rose. Both Sir Alfred
Pease and Major J. Fairfax-Blakeborough made the point
that both Manica and Jalap being so near the roots of
Thoroughbred genealogy will have resembled the original
Oriental type much more than the racehorse of today, or
even of the late 18th-century.

Or the other five Thoroughbred sires known to have contributed to the ancestry of the Cleveland Bay, Bedalian, Ben Ledi, Grog, Molyneux and Muley, none was born later than 1820, and hence no mares can have been covered by them after about 1840. But again, Grog, foaled in 1786, figures more prominently in Yorkshire Coach Horse pedigrees than in those of Cleveland Bays.

The blood of these two famous Oriental sires was conveyed principally through the Cleveland stallions Sportsman 299, foaled in 1876, and Barnaby 21, third of that name, foaled in 1860.

In 1920, owing to the depletion of stock caused by World War I, the breed society opened a register for hitherto unregistered Cleveland mares and for, after inspection by a committee had shown them to be of the old Cleveland type, free of carting blood, some mares already entered in the Yorkshire Coach Horse Stud Book. The progeny of such mares was admitted to competitions and show classes reserved for Cleveland Bays, and their progeny was eligible for entry in the Stud Book proper. Some of these were owned or bred by King George V.

V

PRIVATE COACHING HEYDAY

The expansion of the harness horse and its employment, which — contrary to all expectations — was a direct result of the passenger carrying railway, took some curious forms. Not least of which was the railway line that ran through the heart of the moorlands, from Pickering to Whitby by way of Goathland. It was a complicated bit of engineering, carried out by George Stephenson on a line parallel to the turnpike road which in its turn overlay the ancient pack causeway over Saltersgate Brow that had been trodden by trains of sumpter horses from time immemorial.

The railway followed the bottom of steep-sided, flat-floored Newtondale until the last possible point, so as to cross over into the valley of the Mirk Esk where the watershed was lowest. But this ingenious line was not at first travelled by Stephenson's engines. The rolling stock was of the normal kind, but was drawn by horses: mostly Cleveland Bays. It was, therefore, fitting that when this line, long prostrate as the victim of Beeching, was brought back to active life by a society of dedicated enthusiasts who now operate it as the North York Moors Railway, the Royal personage who performed the re-opening ceremony should have been conveyed to the scene of that ceremony by a team of Cleveland Bays.

Carriage traffic increased enormously, in inverse proportion to the decline of the long distance mail coach, as the railway network expanded. In terms of pure pleasure travelling this is very notable. Resorts of all kinds, once made accessible by rail, began to sprout public coach services, primarily for the custom of those visitors who wished to see more of the district than the town to which the railway brought them. Examples are Bath and Cheltenham; and notably the Lake District with coach services radiating from Keswick; and, nearer the Cleveland heartland, Scarborough. The coach service from there to Bridlington did not exist before the railway line from York to Scarborough was opened, but once the visitors had come, then they must be taken on excursions to Bridlington. In urban areas, the horsedrawn omnibus and the horsedrawn tram proliferated.

So much for public vehicles. But as industrial enterprise spread, so more and more industrialists found themselves obliged to travel in the course of business: in their rise to prosperity they had ceased to live "over the shop" as their fathers had not been too proud to do. They must have a rural or at least suburban residence, out of range of the soot and the coal dust and the industrial muck in which their employees lived and died: and consequently must have a carriage to take them to the mill or the station in the morning and fetch them home at night.

It was the paradox of the Victorian era that whereas in commerce and industry Britain went from strength to strength, the whole reign of the Queen — and indeed most of the extended period between the fall of Napoleon and the Kaiser's War — was one of intermittent agricultural depression, despite the unsurpassed technical superiority of British farming and the high quality of its product. But the prosperity of most farmers does not depend on quality, it depends on a demand for quantity. To feed the rapidly increasing industrial workforce, government policy irrespective of party favoured the importation of cheap grain, of cheap beef on the hoof, of more and more cheap pigmeat and dairy produce as the progress of science made their preservation in bulk for the duration of a sea voyage possible. Fresh milk alone was beyond this technical possibility, and at times dairy farmers within reach of large towns were the only ones who prospered. When the price of wheat fell to 25s a quarter, as it often did, it did not pay the farmer any more to sell it to the millers. It was better to feed it to the pigs; leaving him only the problem of selling pork on the trotter at a profit. But the North Yorkshire farmer had his sheet anchor in bad times. If beef or butter or corn did not pay in the face of imported products, somewhere not far away coal or cotton or worsted or steel was making fortunes; consequently some ironmaster or clothier or weaver, some landowner whose barren acres were bringing him coal royalties galore, was rising fast enough for him to assume the outward and visible sign of prosperity by "setting up a carriage". The good bay mare might be ploughing and harrowing, hauling the ever-increasing seed drills and harvesters to produce a crop that sold for derisory prices: but the crop from the mare herself, in the shape of a four-year-old colt suitable for carriage work, brought its true value in hard cash.

And not from home customers only. The 19th-century saw the greatest expansion abroad of the Cleveland Bay. It is not measurable in terms of Cleveland studs in foreign countries, because the breeding stock sold was used almost exclusively for crossing purposes, and Clevelands are the great upgraders. They were sold not only to the Antipodes, or to South Africa, where no indigenous breeds of horse existed, but to North America, to the Indian sub-continent, and to some European countries. For reasons of national prestige, breeders in some of these countries are shy in acknowledging the improvement that Cleveland sires have made to the quality of their national breed of horse. And for reasons arising from the nature of the international horse trade of that time, they are often honestly vague about the exact origin of the imported stallion. It is, regrettably, often impossible to link the pedigree of the foreign breed with lines of ancestry recorded in the Cleveland Stud Book, though these extend far enough back, in many instances, to antedate the earliest Victorian export boom by a comfortable margin. The cause in most instances lies with the dealer who did the actual shipping, who not only was not English, neither was he a national of the importing country. A classic instance may be found in the Stud Book of the Jutland Horse, a powerful agricultural horse which today resembles the Suffolk more than any other British breed. Jutland breeders admit it owes much to Oppenheim, reputedly a Cleveland Bay, notably its active gait. But Oppenheim cannot be identified in the Cleveland Bay Stud Book because this is simply the name of the Hamburg dealer who bought him at Hull or Howden, and shipped him to Kiel and thence to Denmark. This does not mean that Oppenheim the horse was not a genuine Cleveland Bay, or Yorkshire Coach Horse (or Shire, as some maintain).

The most distant European country to which stallions were exported was Russia. Before the Revolution the Empire of the Tsar contained about fifty recognizable breeds of horses, none of them suitable for heavy draught such as a Clydesdale or a Boulonnais could perform. But, in 1887, Russian breeders in the Vladimir district synthetised a heavy draught breed, now known as the Tractor Horse, on the basis of local mares put to a variety of French and Belgian draught horses, and a Cleveland Bay.

It seemed there would be no end to the agricultural opportunities for a powerful horse like the Cleveland. More (and heavier) tillage machines, haymakers and harvesters came into use. Steam power made surprisingly little inroad on oat-fuelled horsepower. The steam plough — not a tractor, but worked by static engines at either end of a field — never really caught on. Cake crushers and grist mills, powered by horses working a capstan, were installed in circular or hexagonal buildings, the "wheelsheds" of many North Riding farms which, converted to other uses, are their memorial today. The bay horses made them tick. The threshing machine came, so that steam took over the backbreaking toil of the days when husbandmen wielded the flail between the barn doors all winter. But horses hauled them to work, and the coal that fed them.

But it was the American trade that bulked largest in the export field. The American Cleveland Bay Stud Book began publication in 1889, but the entries in it go back to the 1860s. With returning prosperity after the Civil War, great numbers of bay horses were shipped across the ocean; mostly for carriage work, and the American breed society has had a continuous existence since 1889. Most of the imported horses, if entire, were used for cross-breeding. Here too, it is often hard to establish continuity between English and American recorded pedigrees. If a sea-change is suffered, the cause lies again at the doors of dealers who often seem to have been unable to distinguish between a Cleveland Bay and a Yorkshire Coach Horse. But the description, especially of markings, in the American Volume I, seems to indicate the latter rather than the former, in many cases.

By the end of Queen Victoria's reign, there were about 4,000,000 horses in the United Kingdom, of which the vast majority worked in harness. Of these, 300,000 worked in London. (Today, out of less than 1,000,000 British horses and ponies, only a very small minority have ever been between the shafts.) Stud Books for that vast equine population there were none, other than Weatherby's, until late in the

century. Then it began: Shire, Shetland, Hackney, Clydesdale . . . until in 1883 a group of interested persons formed a
project for a Cleveland Bay Stud Book. Its editor, and the
first secretary of the Cleveland Bay Horse Society, was
William Scarth Dixon, a highly professional agricultural,
racing and hunting correspondent, reporter of agricultural
shows for *The Field, The Yorkshire Post, Farmer and Stock
Breeder, Livestock Journal* . . . . you name it, he wrote for it.

Born at Marton in Cleveland in the 1840s, Dixon lived on
into the 1930s, coming as he did of a very long-lived family.
For instance, as a little boy he used to go and visit his
grandmother Scarth, who lived at Stanghow near the
seaward edge of the moors. There he talked to her old
servant Nanny Chapman, then in her ninety-fifth year; her
father had lived to the same age and her grandfather to
almost a hundred. The effect of these long lives laid, not end
to end, but overlapping, was to give young Dixon some
astonishing links with the past. Nanny Chapman in her
girlhood would talk with her grandfather who had lived
through the Civil Wars which ended in 1651, and he told
her much about the adventures of the Scarth family and their
adroit changes of front according to the ups and downs of
the war, whereby they always managed to come out on top.

Such an inheritance, combined with his intimate
knowledge of the countryside, provided Dixon with the ideal
equipment for his task of investigating pedigrees that were a
matter of oral tradition rather than documents. For instance
that notable sire of unknown parentage, the Hob Hill Horse,
had been bought at Yarm Fair to go to Saltburn in 1809,
when Nanny Chapman was already nearly sixty: fresh in the
memory, as it were. As for the documentary side, Sir Alfred
Pease looked after that and with his scholarly method was
able to sort grain from chaff. The Stud Book came out in
1884 and the breed society got under way. Much vital

information about the early days of the breed can be found in the Introductions to its first 15 volumes.

It is remarkable down to what a late date the Cleveland Bays worked, if not in the same teams, at least in the same fields, with draught oxen, mostly of the old Durham breed. When I was an undergraduate I heard the aged Sir Alfred Pease say that he remembered in his youth seeing wagons drawn by oxen in the streets of Saltburn, a mile from the farm where the third and fourth generations of the Hob Hill Horse's descendants were working. And there were no streets at Saltburn until about 1865. Specifically, he said that these ox-wagons came from Moorsholm, which is in sight of Stanghow where Nanny Chapman worked for so long, and also of Gerrick where Mr. Joseph Sunley has his stud of bay mares: the heart of the Cleveland homeland.

Show jumping began in the second half of the Victorian era, after the rules were codified in 1863. Among the topmost performers of those early days were two mares. One, Star, was a purebred Cleveland, bred and owned by a Mr. Duell of Dalehouse, a family still noted among Cleveland breeders. The other was Fanny Drape, owned by Joseph Fearon of Whitehaven. (To have earned this surname, Fanny must have been a conspicuous failure as a brood mare before taking to show jumping. Drape, in the idiom of North Riding butchers and knackers, is a term applied exclusively to cows, and means a barrener, to be fattened for low-quality beef.) She was by a Cleveland Bay stallion and, when competing at the Royal Agricultural Society's show around 1869, she jumped a solid stone wall 6 ft (1 m 85 cms) high, not part of the course. At the Cleveland Show at Middlesbrough the same year she gave a solo exhibition of jumping in hand, clearing a bar estimated to be 7½ ft (2 m 30 cms) high under which her leader ran. One day she attempted the impossible and broke her back.

VI

ENTER A HORSELESS CARRIAGE

The steam engine had failed to knock out the harness horse:
on the contrary it opened new opportunities for it. And so,
when in the Edwardian Age the first automobiles took the
road in town and country, few breeders recognized in them
a serious menace. Not even Cleveland breeders. The horse
was still King of the Road; the Cleveland and its crosses were
the King of the harness horses; traffic regulations were
framed entirely in terms of horsedrawn transport and under
them the motor-car suffered severe disabilities.

In any case, for a long time motor-vehicles were a matter
of private ownership only. Chars-à-bancs (sharabangs) were
still horsedrawn; so were buses; so were trams; so were dust-
carts and bathing machines and reapers-and-binders and
milk floats and ice-cream carts and fire-engines. So too in
the United States, where the number of working horses
reached its peak as late as 1921 (17 million farm horses,
about 5 million others).

Military demands had never played the same part in
Britain among breeders of warm-bloods as they had in
Continental countries. The high prestige of British infantry,
its skill in musketry, and the unchallenged status of the
Royal Navy combined to keep cavalry to the role of a
prestigious supporting arm. But the astonishing feats of the
mounted Boer commandos in the South African War
convinced the War Office that the next war (which of course
would be of the same sort) would be won by mounted

FIGURE 10   A pair of Cleveland Bay horses, in harness to the Ely Fire Engine before 1914. These vehicles were very heavy to pull, but they still had to move fast and only the Cleveland Bay could combine the two requirements; which was also valid for artillery teams.

infantry. And the short-legged sort of Cleveland, about 15 h.h., was just the sort to carry a British trooper with his all-up weight of 18st (115 kgs), while the taller sort of Cleveland was just the sort of horse for the 18 pounder batteries of the Field Artillery and the 13 pounders of the Horse Artillery. So Whitehall not only bought remounts of this stock, it handed out premiums to Cleveland stallions.

When the next war came, it was not at all like Mafeking and all that. But it swallowed up vast numbers of horses, especially artillery horses, and the losses among Clevelands were as high as any. Towards the end of his life, William Scarth Dixon inclined to the view that his researches and those of Sir Alfred Pease had been too thorough, their standards of purity too high, in the 1880s. They had excluded, on grounds of ancestry alone, too many good horses. In 1918, on the Western Front alone, the Allies had lost 47,000 horses a month, though no mounted soldier had come face to face with the enemy. In 1921, stocks being so depleted, the rules were amended to admit to competition as Cleveland Bays, certain animals which would not have been eligible in terms of the original Stud Book, and a register was opened for mares of undeniable Cleveland type to be entered after inspection, their progeny qualifying by stages for admission to the Stud Book proper.

But all the time the demand was shrinking even faster than the supply. Both hunting and steeplechasing picked up and expanded after World War I, but driving did not.

People of my generation, born in the year of Cambrai, the first tank battle ever, can remember the portents. Childhood recollections include some drives in carriages, such as a picnic in a landau hired by my grandfather, but many more in cars, such as trips round the Dales in my uncle's De Dion Bouton and excursions to Mount Grace and Rievaulx in a high-cabbed, brass-horned taxi whose driver still wore a white stock like the coachman he had been. The way was along the Blakey Ridge road, which passes this house a hundred feet nearer the sky, now motorable throughout for two streams of traffic but then single-track, stony, rutted, with a ribbon of grass down the middle. We passed many farmers' gigs drawn in on lay-bys: but for five miles we could not pass a loaded hay-wagon drawn by three horses. This was typical: farmers were still using the Cleveland Bay, but selling it less and less. The Great American Depression of 1930 did the export business no good, and in that year the total number of American horses had dropped by seven million in about nine years to just under 15 million. The horse-drawn sharabang, once the only vehicle for summer outings, was gone before our time: the earliest I can recall,

FIGURE 11   A Cleveland Bay stallion, Grange Lad, in hand between the two World Wars. Here appearing taller than in reality, as the short leader stands beyond him.

full of joyous trippers from Bradford or Gateshead, were by Foden out of Leyland. Only politicians, and some serving Generals who should have known better, continued to talk about the Role of the Horse in War as if the tank and the armoured car, the landmine and the low-level bomber, had never been invented. This sort of talk went on right up to the Spanish Civil War.

The effects of Hitler's war were not so dire for the Cleveland as for some other breeds, because so many of them qualified as agricultural workers entitled to appropriate rations. But in the wake of that war mechanization came to the farms, even the moorland farms, by slow stages and what the motor-car had spared the tractor finished off.

The decline was still slow, but unfaltering, and it quickened after 1950. In 1960 the nadir of misfortune was reached, when at last the War Office discontinued its premiums to stallions. Many owners ceased to breed from their mares, but in those days of comparative affluence did not feel compelled to put them down.

VII

NOW

By now is meant, not simply the Olympic Year of Montreal, the last in which Jack Fairfax-Blakeborough, M.C., M.B.E. lived among us; the hundredth since Sportsman was foaled; the two hundredth since the American Declaration of Independence, and the birth of my grandfather's grandfather Dent, and the year (probably) in which Jalap covered a mare for the last time; the three hundredth since Whitby men built, and before evacuation demolished, the Mole of Tangier, and Whitby ships brought Barb stallions home to Cleveland.

We mean rather the seventies in general and the late sixties. The years between 1945 and 1965 had seen a great upsurge in the popularity of ponies, and not only children's ponies but such as adults might also ride. This began in Britain but spread to the Low Countries, to Germany, to Scandinavia and France. At the same time there was a renewed and growing interest in Arabian horses in the same region, in North America and what has become known as the White Commonwealth. This resulted, in Britain, in a population explosion of part-bred Arabs, predominantly ponies. The result has been that the average riding horse is much lighter all round than it was before 1939. But at the same time the average height and weight of Europeans has been, and is, speedily, increasing.

Sooner or later a demand for saddle horses of more substance was bound to be felt, and during the last ten years the problem of supply has become more and more acute.

Riding horses of more substance are now being bred by means of the Cleveland cross which adds solidity and strength without loss of quality (and incidentally the converse is true: the same cross will impart quality to a coarser breed without loss of substance or toughness).

Two factors militate in favour of the Cleveland Bay as a sire of hunters. One is the enthusiastic, but not always well-advised, use by amateur breeders, of the Hunter Improvement Society premium stallions. This service has the fatal advantage of accessibility, and as the cost of transport rises the temptation to turn to the nearest sire is strong. The result has been that there are by now a great many hunter mares that are something like seven-eighths bred: the other eighth can have been anything, but is more likely than not to have had pony blood. This is not necessarily a good recipe, nor would it be even if the average owner, pedigree apart, were to analyse seriously the make and shape of his mare to see whether they complemented that of the Hunter Improvement Society sire, and vice versa. Of course in principle a blood horse will get a good hunter off a halfbred mare: but not any such horse off any such mare — the two individuals must be compatible. Even so, the warning uttered by Sir Alfred Pease fifty years ago is still valid today: "Breeding hunters off hunter mares is a lottery and it is doubtful, when you consider all the qualities which go to make a good hunter: bone, agility, courage, strength, pace, cleverness, conformation, eye, stamina, temperament and natural aptitude for leaping, if they can ever be combined in a fixed hunter breed." That is a formidable list of desired characteristics, not more than half of which one could reasonably expect to derive from the sire.

As to the seven-eighths mare, the last word in breeding from her must rest with that great-granddam of unknown

FIGURE 12   A two-year-old filly at grass.

origin, who probably lived and died within the last fifty years or less, but about whom the owner of the mare probably knows less than I do about one of my great-grandmothers whose photograph happens to have survived. But this old lady without a pedigree may well have been as prepotent, for good or ill, as my great-grandmother (1810-1869) whose features I have seen looking out at me not once but many times over from the faces of my cousins' children. Even at the range of four generations her genetic heritage may yet prevail over those of the other seven forbears of her generation; even though the daughters and granddaughters in between may not have favoured her.

But then, some people *like* lotteries.

Whereas the full-blooded Cleveland is strongly prepotent and genetically stable: or to put it more succinctly in traditional language, breeds true.

It is not only genetically stable but emotionally stable. The Cleveland temperament is calm and equable, unflappable. But just as great numbers of light (too light) horses bred since 1945 have inherited a certain lightness of bone and narrowness of body through ill-chosen admixture of Arab or near-Arab or Thoroughbred blood, they have inherited also the dark side of hot-blooded psychology and are of a more volatile temperament than is desirable in, say, a hunter. A Cleveland sire or a half-Cleveland dam tends to ensure progeny that uses its head and takes its time in confronting obstacles in the hunting field or on the event course or in the show jumping ring.

Of course, occasional instances of impetuosity have been known: for instance, Peter Simple, who was out of a part-Cleveland mare, ran in the Grand National starting at 6 to 1 and carrying 12 stone. His jockey could not hold him and was discarded, only to catch Peter Simple and mount again. But they still finished third, within six lengths of the winner,

FIGURE 13 A successful show jumper, North Flight, is a cross between a Cleveland Bay and a Thoroughbred. Owned by David and William Barker, he competed in the Tokyo Olympics.

Gaylad. The moral of this story is that not only the second cross, but even the first cross Cleveland, is good enough to run in the world's most famous steeplechase, and probably good enough to win it, because surely it takes longer for a man to catch a horse and get up than for a horse to run six times its own length.

More typical of the deliberate Cleveland temperament which is a useful asset in competitive jumping, are David and William Barker's successful show jumpers North Flight *(Figure 13)* and Newsham Bell, both half-Cleveland Bays.

The other factor is the absence of an English alternative. Traditionally, the basis of hunter breeding in Britain, on the dams side, has been the Irish Draught mare who imparted, to a foal by a Thoroughbred, natural jumping ability, depth and width of body. But the reservoir of these useful animals has been sadly drained of late years, as the mechanization of Irish farming proceeded, and the European horsemeat trade has made large inroads on it. The Irish Department of Agriculture has now started a Register (not as yet a Stud Book) of Irish Draught Horses, but this measure will not of itself increase numbers, though it will ensure authenticity (a mare is not necessarily Irish Draught because an English dealer bought her in Limerick and she will go in a cart, whereas a Cleveland Bay is a Cleveland Bay, whether foaled in Kentucky or New South Wales.)

The Cleveland Bay breed has latterly come into the public eye through its representatives in the Royal Mews, notably when they are being driven in competitive events by the Duke of Edinburgh. But in fact such patronage is no new thing. Without going back to the days of George II, it is sufficient to mention that Volume XVI of the Cleveland Bay Stud Book listed 26 horses and mares in the Register owned and/or bred by King George V, and five in the main body of the book, in the 1920s.

FIGURE 14   Two of H.M. The Queen's part-bred Cleveland
Bays at Windsor Castle.

To judge by the state of the breed today, nobody would guess that sixteen years ago it had stood on the edge of the abyss. Hardly had the War Office withdrawn its patronage when the newly formed Horse-Race Betting Levy Board stepped in with the same subvention that it extends to all recognised associations of horse-breeders. This grant is not only drawn from a more logical source of supply (who can pretend, in this age, that horses have anything to do with war, or training for it?) since it is not, in the normal sense, public money but a percentage of the money which members of the public have already spent on pleasure by gambling it away; but it is also allocated in a more realistic way. Within very wide limits, the breed society can spend the grant on promotion of breeding in whatever way it sees fit. Whereas the War Office simply paid the sum of £30 to every stallion that had covered 15 mares in the past season, the Society can spend the grant on premiums at stallion parades; or in grants for pure-bred foals; or in travel allowances for taking pure-bred stock to shows of national importance at a distance from their home — whichever seems more opportune from time to time.

In the 1960s, the wheels began to turn again. The exceptional longevity of the Cleveland helped the revival. Mares which had not been bred from for many seasons were put to the horse again, and proved fertile. In some cases much patient research had to be done to establish the identity of mares which, on investigation, proved to be of undoubted authentic pedigree. The owners might have been spared this trouble if the system, so widespread in Europe, of providing registered stock with an indelible means of identification had been adopted. In Britain, only the Exmoor Pony Society practises it: but at least two instances in our time have proved its value in a crisis. In Spain, after the devastation and dispersals of the Civil War, it was only possible to reconstitute the famous Arabian studs of the Duke of Veragua and the Yeguada Militar by means of their brands; so it was in West Germany also, after the evacuation of East Prussia and the migration, on foot, of the nucleus of the Trakehnen stud to the West away from the Russian encirclement. In the latter country, stallions and mares with the renowned elk-antler brand were found pulling ploughs and doing much more menial tasks than that, and brought back into breeding activity. The Cleveland revival may not have had the dramatic quality of, say, General Patton's counter-kidnapping of the unique Lipizzan breeding herd and its repatriation from Bohemia to Austria: but for all that, this reversal of the trend of affairs at the last moment had about it the elements of a rescue operation.

The public, especially the large spectator public for show jumping, is nowadays much more aware of the prevalence of Cleveland blood in show jumpers and event horses of the first rank. Besides the two mentioned above, examples that come to mind are Harvey Smith's Madison Time, a part-Cleveland who competed for the British team in the Mexico Olympics; Rembrandt, out of a half-bred Cleveland mare, by a Thoroughbred, who in the late 1960s won several national three-day events; Viscount, likewise out of a half-Cleveland mare, with a similar record to the above in the same years; Island Monarch, by Happy Monarh (Thoroughbred) out of a Cleveland mare, competing in three-day events in 1976, having come sixth at Osberton in 1975; Pistol Pete, by Speculation who was by a Thoroughbred out of a Cleveland Bay mare. He was Reserve with the Canadian show jumping team at the Montreal Olympic games; Sumatra, another horse by the same sire, was sole Canadian representative at the World Championship event, Burghley, 1974, gaining 8th place.

The last two were bred in Canada, where there is not much breeding of pure Clevelands, but an increasing amount of cross-breeding. The same is true of the United States, where there is a great deal of "submerged" Cleveland blood, among hunters and event horses, especially in the Atlantic seaboard states and those parts of the South where "English pleasure" riding and fox hunting more or less in the English tradition are prevalent.

Exports in general have for a long time now been overseas rather than to the Continent of Europe. In Australia and New Zealand the produce of Cleveland Bay stallions out of country-bred mares is much sought after for work on sheep and cattle stations. The imperial household of Japan has long been a steady customer, and in the period in question has bought six purebred Clevelands and some half-breds. Australia and the United States continue to import.

At home, the scene has been transformed by the number and distribution of Cleveland stallions standing at stud. Outside Yorkshire, 24 are now to be found in 15 English counties: there is one in North Wales, one in South Wales, two in the Scottish Lowlands and two in the Highlands, and there is one in the Isle of Man. Seven now stand in Yorkshire. Yet in 1960 there were only four in the whole country.

Progress made during the decade is measurable, for instance, by the annual sales at Wetherby in May and October. At the May sale in 1969 there were six times as many lots forward as in 1966, and many more foals came forward at the October sales. Next year five stallions competed for the King George V Cup, awarded to the Champion Stallion of the breed, whereas ten years earlier there had not been five stallions in the country. Ever since then there have been more classes for Cleveland Bays at horse shows, and better filled, both at North Country

FIGURE 15   A typical 1970s stallion at stud.

fixtures from the Great Yorkshire downwards, and at national exhibitions like the Royal at Stoneleigh.

Here, is perhaps the place to add that for those genuinely interested in the breed, including intending purchasers, the best observation post is perhaps not a show like the Royal or the Great Yorkshire at Harrogate, but some smaller affair held in the heart of the breeding area. The reason is that many of the best breeders are farmers, busy men and short-handed, who simply have not the time to float away to Warwickshire or even to Harrogate. Try the Ryedale at Kirbymoorside, or Danby or Stokesley or Hinderwell or Egton — an interesting affair, a notable venue also for heavy horses, the successor in title to a horse fair founded by ancient charter.

Now

Look not only at the entries in the breed classes themselves but also at the hunter classes and see how many you can identify in the latter, as being out of Cleveland or half-Cleveland mares. There will also be many brood mares with foals by Cleveland Bays at foot.

VIII

TOMORROW

To prophesy is to invite the derision of the next generation
in due course, but let me attempt some forecast of the future
of the Cleveland Bay nevertheless. It may best be done by
trying to observe some pattern in the past history of the
breed and, if it is a recurring one, to estimate when it is
likely to repeat itself. But first let us observe that horse-
breeders and those to whom their product is sold tend to be
of a conservative temper, at any rate with a small "c".
Fashion exists in the horse world, but except in the most
superficial and trivial matters it tends to change very slowly.
"Progress" in the material sense can be ruled out, because
horses of all kinds have ceased to play a part in our
economy, whether in agriculture or in transport or in
industry (for reasons of space I have virtually omitted, in the
preceding chapters, any mention of the part Cleveland Bays
played in the mining and metallurgical industry of the
region: but it was a considerable one).

   Looking back, it seems to me that major new departures
in the Cleveland Bay's progress only occur about once in a
hundred years, and in the first quarter of the century. If you
reckon 1620 for the introduction of the first Duke of
Buckingham's Spanish stallions; 1720 for the consolidation
of the Thoroughbred as a breed and the parting of the ways
between it and the Cleveland Bay, each taking away, in
different directions, that part of their ancestry which they
had in common; 1820, or somewhat later, for the advent of

the railway and the decline of long-distance coach traffic; 1920 for the irreversible triumph of the motor-car: then the next major change is indicated at around the year 2020. My 105th birthday would fall in that year but many of my readers will still be sitting in the saddle or on the box then. Now to take a cross-bearing on the contemporary trend, it does seem as if the recent revival in harness matters, if it has any considerable life in it, will last about a century and should still be full of running in 2020. Nor is it very likely that a better foundation for coaching stock will be found in the British Isles, whether they are still a United Kingdom or a Federation of People's Republics, both for competitive sport and for state occasions. So that in the next century we may look to see Cleveland Bays competing in the harness events of the Pan-British Games held at the holy and permanently neutral venue of Newmarket whose integrity has been respected by all combatant states even during the years that separate the sexennial Games. While the state coaches of the Protector of the English Commonwealth, the Lord Governor of Scotland, the Regent of Ulster and the President of Wales will be drawn in procession all by Cleveland Bays. Only the President of Eire will make his stately progress behind a team of Irish Draught stallions.

Assuming that fox hunting is still legal in at least some part of the said islands by then, the proportion of hunters with at least some Cleveland Bay blood is likely to exceed the present one, because the trend mentioned in the last chapter for people to grow taller and heavier is almost certain to continue, and may well accelerate. It is unlikely that the vogue for light, *light* horses of the years 1950-1970 will recur, and if the pursuit of live game with hounds is banned by the laws of the future, the same major part will be played by Cleveland or part-Cleveland horses in the horse-trials and mock-hunts that will replace it, as has been played

FIGURE 16   A shepherd at work on the moorland, mounted on
a Cleveland Bay which is the ideal horse in such country.

in the hunting field over the past three centuries.

In short, the Cleveland Bay will remain the grown-up
horse for grown-up people.

As a demonstration of how to forecast things to come by
looking into the past, we cannot do better than . . . .

IX

.... ASK THE OLD MEN

"Young men scarcely recollect nice mouldy sorts
before the railways knocked packing off the roads."
Lumley Hodgson

When the Cleveland Bay Horse Society was formed in 1883 the Stud Book Editing Committee had the idea of asking the oldest surviving breeders for a general background of information that would supplement written records on such matters as prices and performance, besides the purely genealogical facts as to who begat what. Of these informants the most articulate, the best informed and the most forthright was Lumley Hodgson, farmer and breeder, some time of Northallerton but latterly of Easingwold. He was then seventy-six years of age, having been born two years after the Battle of Trafalgar.

His trenchant remarks should be taken with only one reservation, which will be more obvious to those of my readers who like myself can say *"J'ai passé la cinquantaine"*, or more. As one walks down the far slope of the hill of summers, nothing is ever quite as good as "when I were a lad". The beer does not taste so good, the horses don't go so well, the women . . . .

Hodgson lamented "the great injury foreigners have done to the breed of horses in taking away the old breed of Chapman, or as they have latterly been called, Cleveland Bays." He recalled great feats of time past such as "old Mr.

Maynard riding his horse Black Tommy from Highthorne to Newcastle, forty miles without a bait, swimming the Tees at night . . . . " or "old Tommy Miles of Harlsey, riding the same mare from Harlsey to have his name called every morning in the Court at York, and home to sleep in his own bed every night for a week, rested on Sunday, did the same thing on Monday."

His ideal — the old Chapman sort — was never above 15½ h.h., for the very good reason that a packhorse taller than this is more difficult to load and unload, and until he was forty years old "packing" was still a daily necessity to people living away from the railway and the wagonnable roads: and in the great triangle of moorland intersected by fertile dales between Pickering and Yarm and Whitby there were no such roads though this area was bordered by "turnpike" carriageways. A year before Hodgson's letters, Canon Atkinson of Danby had written that up to 1847 "many tons of coal have been brought into this district" (out of County Durham) "in long narrow sackes or 'pokes' holding about 2 cwt each on the backs of horses in gangs of 25 or 30. All the traffic into or out of the district was then conducted by 'panniermen'". Hodgson says, speaking of the short stretches of "parish" road that *were* suitable for heavy wheeled traffic "in Cleveland and the Dales you seldom saw any real Cart horses used" (he means Clydesdale or Shire or Old Black) "and constantly met 8 or 10 teams in the Dales leading stones with 2 or 3 in each cart or wagon — all bays with black legs. To a Thoroughbred sire they bred the finest Carriage horses and hunters according to the shape of sire and dam." He mentions, as purebred coaching sires, the Hob Hill Horse, Roseberry, Old Forester, and many others, down to the last of the race, old Salesman whom he bred himself. "Flashy coach horses that spoiled the present breed", too high on the leg, too long in the back he does not scruple to name, either. They all came from Holderness.

As to prices ruling in his youth he recalls selling three-year-olds of his own breeding for £70 to £120, unbroken: four-year-old mares for £105 and four-year-old horses for £120 to £180. His top price was a halfbred colt by Perion for £250 "to go abroad". All these prices he reckoned paid him, but to sell a horse for £60 was "fooling it away". A blood hunter then cost about 400 guineas.

As to numbers: "When I was young you used to meet hundreds of nice mouldy mares in strings of 8 to 10 tied together all the way up the road from Northallerton to London, such as you don't see ten of in a year, now."

And source of supply: "Forty or fifty years ago I could have gone into Cleveland and the Dales and could have bought twenty such colts and horses as you cannot find now, without spending more than you would" (pay for one now). "This was a most valuable breed when I was young in the hands of nearly every farmer in Yorkshire, especially in Cleveland and the Moor Dales — Bilsdale, Rosedale, Egton, Farndale, Westerdale, Danby, and all about Whitby and Pickering. I started farming with three such old-fashioned Chapman mares, to farm and breed from, as you would have some trouble to find now, regardless of price."

Since he very rarely mentions dates we may give, as landmarks in his time scale "When I Was Young": this means before Queen Victoria came to the throne; and "When I Started Farming" — about 1829. But he really thought of horses, and his life — the same thing — as either before or after the railways. This deadline was the year 1825, when he was eighteen.

Who were the "foreigners", who share the blame in his eyes with the railways, for the decline of the breed? They need not necessarily have been Rooshians, Frenchmen or Prooshians, or Eyetalians either. They may well have

FIGURE 17 The nightmare of Lumley Hodgson's youth — a "Fiery Steed". From an original engraving by G. Cruickshank, 1829.

included a miserable, almost sub-human race domiciled South of the Humber. His England is like the England of an Upper Teesdale farmer, a patient of my grandfather (born 1851), who once told about the prowess of his mare: "A grand galloway is that, Mr. Dent. She wan t'fost prize at Bowes Show, and they come from all ower England ti Bowes Show — Kendal, Sedbergh, Kirby Stephen — aye, all ower England."

Even Hodgson's Yorkshire is similarly restricted. When he says "nearly every farmer in Yorkshire" he really means the eastern and central parts of the county — not the Pennine parts of the West Riding, nor Richmondshire in the North Riding, which are sheep and dairy country, not arable. But he is undoubtedly right when he says "before railways, people from all parts of England came down to York and Northallerton Fairs to buy them."

The railways strangled the mail coach business stone dead in about fifteen years: rigor mortis had set in when he was 33. As he said, it scared the breeders, because everybody thought that the next stage would be road going steam carriages. But this was not to be. Instead of horses vanishing from the road, a new, vastly increased and quite different type of carriage trade developed, demanding a different sort of horse, and involving only short journeys. More and more people had to be got to and from the station — the poor as cheaply as possible, the rich at speed, if possible in splendour. As early as the 1790s the London and export carriage trade had swallowed up the rejects of Cleveland breeding, as we may read in William Marshall's *Rural Economy of Yorkshire*, where he says that the taller, leggier, cross-bred sorts from the Vale of Pickering and the Plain of York were eagerly bought by outsiders. This was still the case, but now not only were some farmers deliberately breeding such "seconds" to meet the demands of an easy market, but purebred stock too was being sold out of the country.

Among the foreign buyers were Dutch and German dealers who landed at Hull and probably never went further up the country than Howden. Many were agents for the State Studs of various countries: which is to say for the remount farms of their respective armies. No government of that period made any attempt to tamper with the sacred cow, Free Enterprise, or to ensure that good breeding stock did not fall into the hands of governments unfriendly to us. No one will ever know how many Green Howards, how many Durham Light Infantrymen, how many Northumberland Fusiliers between 1914 and 1918 were blown to pieces by the fire of guns that were hauled into action by teams sired by

Cleveland Bays. This is the more curious since every English monarch from Athelstan to Henry VIII had enacted stringent laws against the sale to foreigners of what was in effect a munition of war. Henry's daughter Mary declined to re-enact them when she married the reigning King of Spain: not wishing to offend her husband's subjects, but yet unwilling to discriminate in their favour. And since her time those laws have never been revived.

Lumley Hodgson's picture was a true and valuable one, if we only discount this one factor — the golden glow of youth seen in retrospect. But so we must in every age. I have no doubt that a senior contemporary giving evidence in 1783 would have lamented tht the breed had been declining for years, that things were never the same after Manica and Jalap stopped getting foals, and that no living horse in Cleveland could match the sort their parents had seen when the Duke of Buckingham hunted from Helmsley Castle. And a similar witness, testifying in 1683, would have said things were never so good since the War between the King and Parliament as before, and worse after the war's end, with all those unemployed Colonels and their Spanish horses driving out the good old breed. And the old men of 1583 would have complained that one did not see "the same good stamp of horse about nowadays such as the White Fathers of Rieveaulx bred before King Harry pulled the roof off their house, God rest their souls, but don't tell parson I said so."

Likewise in 1983 I shall be boring the pants off an audience too young to contradict me when I tell them about the splendid horses with which Cleveland swarmed when I was a lad, and that what they think is a good Cleveland cannot compare with what I saw when Squire Wharton, Master of the Cleveland Hounds, was at Skelton Castle, God was in his heaven and all was right with the world. This despite the fact that the 1930s were years of miserable

FIGURE 18   Mares and foals at the foot of the moor.

economic uncertainty for the North Country, when agriculture was as depressed as mining or ironworking. But whereas in the chronic agricultural depressions of the pre-1914 era Cleveland farmers had always been able to get some ready money by selling a colt off their good bay mares, the motor-car had done for them this time, and seemingly for good. "When I were a lad" very often the only thing that brought ready money into Cleveland farms, not at a loss, was the magnificent ham and egg teas, with cheese cake and plum cake and a dozen other specialities purveyed by farmers' wives to what we then called hikers, at half a crown a time. But I shall have forgotten that. And even while I am pontificating about the decadence of the breed my subject itself will be giving me the lie. If it is winter, somewhere across the black moorland bay horses will be following the hounds as boldly and as cleverly as ever they did in Lumley Hodgson's or the Duke of Buckingham's day. If it is summer, in some green dale beside some beck that runs down into the Esk or the Derwent, solid bay mares will be suckling big-boned foals that will live to gallop on into the twentyfirst century.

Danby-in-Cleveland
1976/1977